Always Room for Interpretation

poems by

Deborah Rasmussen

Finishing Line Press
Georgetown, Kentucky

Always Room for Interpretation

Copyright © 2025 by Deborah Rasmussen
ISBN 979-8-89990-051-8 First Edition
All rights reserved under International and Pan-American Copyright Conventions. No part of this book may be reproduced in any manner whatsoever without written permission from the publisher, except in the case of brief quotations embodied in critical articles and reviews.

ACKNOWLEDGMENTS

I am grateful to the members of my poetry groups for their support and honest commentary, to the welcoming writing community in Duluth of which I am part, and to my husband for his ongoing encouragement. I thank the editors of the following journals who selected some of these poems for publication:

Barstow & Grand: "What the River Did"
Lake Superior Writers Website: "Post-Pandemic" with a different title
Rattle Poets Respond ®: "Speaking of Stable Geniuses"
The Talking Stick: "Danish Dumplings," "Topographies," "Under the Covers on New Year's Day," "Snapshot of My Mother on Vacation," "The Perfect Time for Rain," and an earlier version of "Linguistics"
The Thunderbird Review: an earlier version of "High School Orchestra Performs *The Moldau* by Bedrich Smetana," "Two Moose Cross a Northern Minnesota Lake," and "Always Room for Interpretation."

Publisher: Leah Huete de Maines
Editor: Christen Kincaid
Cover Art: Geoffrey S. Gates
Author Photo: Geoffrey S. Gates
Cover Design: Elizabeth Maines McCleavy

Order online: www.finishinglinepress.com
also available on amazon.com

Author inquiries and mail orders:
Finishing Line Press
PO Box 1626
Georgetown, Kentucky 40324
USA

Contents

The Perfect Time for Remembering 1

Danish Dumplings 2

Linguistics 3

Topographies 4

What the River Did 5

Two Moose Cross a Northern Minnesota Lake 6

Snapshot of My Mother on Vacation 7

High School Orchestra Performs *The Moldau*
    by Bedrich Smetana 8

Still Life of Dad in Rhubarb Bed 9

Post-Pandemic 10

Speaking of Stable Geniuses 11

Going Back 12

Under the Covers on New Year's Day 14

To My Husband Far from Home 15

The Inevitable Time for Dense Fog 16

The Perfect Time for Rain 17

The Perfect Time to Shovel Snow 18

The Perfect Time to Spot an Owl 19

The Perfect Time to Take Down Christmas Lights 20

The Imperfect Time for Brilliant Sunshine 21

Always Room for Interpretation 22

for Geoffrey
48 years and counting

The Perfect Time for Remembering

is when summer's heat finally breaks, rain
kneads away its weight, smooths raw edges
to silk against your skin, softens rough air
the way well-worked dough turns satin in
tender hands, the way flour, yeast, oil, water
become bread, each holding the others
in one unbreakable whole.

Danish Dumplings

There was nothing we called Danish
except the dumplings my grandmother made for soup.
They floated
          like clouds in the painting over her sofa

of green-gold grass, square-fenced and parted
by an empty road where people, I imagined,
walked to the horizon and sailed away in ships
to distant futures, one of which became
my grandmother's. She brought her husband,
two daughters and a landscape from the old country.
Little else
          and rarely spoke of Denmark,

never uttered a word of its tongue in my presence,
just hung its portrait in a prominent place
and made dumplings to fill me with

                  something Danish.

Linguistics

I suspose, Grampa said when
I asked if I could ride Tom,
the old work horse who put up with me
on his back as Grampa led him
around the barn once, twice.
I suspose, he agreed, patient
when I begged for a third round.

No one else said that of course but
I liked the sound of it, didn't care
if there was one S too many. I thought it
an Old Country keepsake,
a Danish dumpling afloat
in the New World soup he ate
once off the boat
missing home
working hard
to raise poultry & kids in Illinois –
chickens to feed the children
he'd vowed to educate
into better lives than farming.

Two teachers & a lawyer
were the harvest of his handiwork
all of whom forgot
the language of their father's heart
but spoke perfect English
which made him proud
I suspose.

Topographies

My father never mentioned the soil
that years ago
released our family roots
from the Danish landscape
never told
how it ached from the pulling
but hid its pain in silence
like his own

when his firstborn
relinquished tender roots
to the will of water
leaving behind
another ruptured landscape
whose soil too
was never mentioned.

What the River Did

It was my job above all
to live, mine and my brother's,
the one who didn't die
stepping over slick stones
into the river that wanted him
as much as our mother did.
From an early age I knew
she couldn't bear another child's death
and couldn't take water lightly.
Innocence would never fool her again
as it had that sweet spring day
when he came into her kitchen for a doughnut,
went out again leaving the goodbye
that would forge her future
the way a hammer pounds red hot iron
into forms that are only altered
by further fire
can never be tempered
by water.

Two Moose Cross a Northern Minnesota Lake

She navigates
toward me
calf behind
plucky
like the kid I was
before sense set in.
Talk, I think,
let her know
where you are.
As I do
a miracle veers away.
I stand safe
sorry
for every want
I never dared
pursue.

Snapshot of My Mother on Vacation

She sits by the pool
as we kids splash & squeal
at some roadside motel
after a long day's drive.

She's vigilant
in a 50s deck chair—
red metal, blazing hot,
just springy enough
to exit quickly—
a lifeguard
in casual travel dress
comfortable shoes
rolled down stockings.

She can't swim
but always watches
because that distant river
still runs through her, the one
carrying her firstborn
farther and farther from home.

**High School Orchestra Performs *The Moldau*
by Bedrich Smetana**

As the curtain rises
I straddle my cello

ride it
like a gleaming horse to water

plunge

into a river
of surging strings
brass
woodwind

pour melody
over roiling rhythm

swirl & sway
to a cadence
that carries me

beyond my banks.

Still Life of Dad in Rhubarb Bed

He stands alone & somber, garden clippers
in one hand, the other at ease on his hip as he
reviews the rhubarb one late-summer day.

He knows what to do—stalks gone to ground,
leaves wilted—it's time to lay another season
to rest, yet he lingers over its remains, visible,

undeniable ruin at his feet. Underground, roots
bear another year's grief, silently remember
to live. Somewhere among the remains of his

87 years there's an older photo of Dad, dressed
in Navy Blue, 1942, smiling beside his bride
for a final shot before he ships out, one of

a hundred raw recruits, brothers by then, trained
& ready. Only two came back—worn, wilted,
unexpectedly alive in an unrecognizable world

where Dad remembered to live, went on to teach
history to high schoolers, tend family, work hard &
raise rhubarb, whose wordless ways he understood.

Post-Pandemic

Wary as a groundhog
I dissect stray shadows
for signs of safety, cling
to the edges of home
envy my rhubarb which
after months underground
bares its face to fickle
sun and capricious snow
brazenly singing sweet
freedom as though this year
might burst into flower.

Speaking of Stable Geniuses

I've only known one. It was my uncle
the dairyman who taught me to dip one finger
into a pail of freshly drawn milk and offer it
to syrup-eyed calves who sucked greedily
for small reward then followed my hand
into the pail over and over until they learned
that milk could be freely lapped!
a miracle in the eyes of us youngsters
and genius, I thought, on the part of my uncle
who called all his look-alike Holsteins by name
and taught each one which slot was her own
among identical stalls in the milking stable.
It was he who could find a calf newly dropped
in the field where its mother thought it well-hidden
and it was he who could stand outside
the barn door and call toward the outer pasture
come boss to bring the herd home safe.
All this I thought to be genius
but I never heard him say so.
He just quietly did his work.

Going Back

The old farmhouse is gone.
Only a slab remains where
I spent summers with Mona,
aunt & able farm woman.

In mid-August we laid table
for the haying crew who'd
show up precisely at noon
to eat egg salad, ham or beef
between generously buttered
squares of dense white bread,
halved & stacked on matching
oval platters. We made tart
lemonade & sweet iced tea,
chopped home-grown spuds
for salad, drew pan after pan
of cookies from the oven,
brewed coffee & set chairs
around the table—8 in all

to put up my uncle's hay.
My grampa drove a tractor
back & forth hoisting bales
4 at a time to the loft where
my brother Jim stood by
with Marvin, the hired man,
to haul them in. There were
2 Rosenbooms—Russ, who
brought his baler & Louie,
our down-the-road-a-ways
neighbor. Heinie Heinrich
farmed over-toward-town,
Goldy Goldtrap arrived by
tractor, hay wagon in tow –
fellow farmers whose fields
the crew worked one by one
till everyone's crop was in.

They strode into our kitchen
on the hour, took turns over
the scrubbed white sink, dried
rough hands on a roller towel,
then sat to eat, filling the air
with farm news like batting
into the community quilt. I
refilled glasses, passed platters
& added my two cents, proud
that no one expected less.

It's all gone now—baler, tractors,
wagon, barn, hayloft, farmers,
cooks & kitchen. Nothing left.
Just a foundation to stand on.

Under the Covers on New Year's Day

The house, like me,
tries to find
a comfortable position.

All our joints creak
as we stretch
into new ways of being

this first morning
of the year
each of us growing older

both wondering
just how long
blood can flow through mortal veins,

water through worn
pipes, how long
aging skeletons can rise

to greet mornings
till, as one,
we sigh, house and I, to see

the ancient sun
do its job
one more day. *There's hope,* I say,

roll over, doze,
as my house
resettles without comment.

To My Husband Far from Home

In your absence there is quiet.
And there is quiet.

The first, an end to conversation
and to your footsteps

going away and coming back
toward me. An end to

the opening of doors by you.
Also their closings.

An end to the kitchen commotion
you make, the music

of plates, pots, silverware stilled
for now. This quiet

settles comfortably over me.
I fall asleep to it

but wake to that other, louder,
quiet: the absence

of breathing beside me at night,
the missing heartbeat

whose sound I still hear
echoing in my own.

The heart, it seems, can hear
what ears only wish for.

The Inevitable Time for Dense Fog

is when you're almost home,
driving uphill toward first view
of Lake Superior which always
makes you smile & you're set
to smile now when fog rolls in,
fast, over terrain you've always
trusted—like at the famous clinic
where you learned his should-be-
simple problem isn't & fog clouds
everything you thought you knew.
Now all you know for sure is
you'll have to drive with care,
hope that home is still ahead &
if you can find it, you'll be safe.

The Perfect Time for Rain

is the morning after your long drive
home from the famous clinic where

even if all went well and they said
there's nothing new to worry about

you know that worries show up like
ticks on innocuous summer days when

you walk the well-mown trail, trousers
tucked into socks tucked into boots,

long-sleeved shirt cinched tight inside
durable denim, cuffs snug, collar up,

broad brimmed hat in place, repellent
close at hand because you know how

new worries will always find you
no matter what the experts say, how

new worries latch on, seen or not, how
only the weeping sky understands.

The Perfect Time to Shovel Snow

is while it's still falling
before the full mass
hits ground & freezes

like when you have to admit
his cancer won't go away,
words you know will grow
heavier over time so you
ration your strength
to face in increments
what you can't change

the way you face a blizzard
shovelful by shovelful
before its weight buries you.

The Perfect Time to Spot an Owl

is one mid-winter afternoon while
chickadees & squirrels tend their work

as though nothing has unsettled the air,
no threat hovers, like when you open

your email, learn that a cousin you love
has had a major stroke, lies in capable

hands, holding on to life for now. You turn
away from the words, notice how outside

the air that upholds life is still there
but nothing is breathing now that

the unchangeable has happened &
the world skews a little more toward death

even if busy critters don't see that owl
watching them—hungry maybe –

maybe not—biding its time in a space
too close for comfort.

The Perfect Time to Take Down Christmas Lights

is late January when winter begins
to waver so slightly you barely notice
new slivers of daylight but sense that
somehow, something has changed

like when you hear there may be
promising new treatment for him
at the famous clinic, feel a nudge
of unexpected hope. You're grateful

but wary because you know how
promises shift, the way daylight swells
only to ebb again. Still, you'll keep
those festive bulbs safe just in case

by chance, there will be reason
to light them one more time.

The Imperfect Time for Brilliant Sunshine

is this April morning after a three-day gale
hurled sleet against windows & drove snow
into spruces already bearing too much. Today,
sun or not, that wind still shrieks, ice still grips
battered shrubs & hedges but now the landscape
glitters in unabashed glee as if to flaunt the ruin
left behind: bent trunks, strewn needles, broken
boughs, tattered bark, his persistent cancer –

okay, you know wind isn't to blame for that but
rage is rage so you rail on behalf of mistreated
trees which, to your surprise, have begun to leak
sunlight through supple branches, shed snow, re-
collect strength, muster resilience & face forward,
making room among their stubborn roots for you.

Always Room for Interpretation

I'm pushing seventy-five
he grumbles, as though at it
for centuries, doomed
as the man in the myth.

That we're still pushing
is the wonder of it, I say
shoulder to my own rock
eyes on the summit

no hurry to get there, not
even sure I will, but keen
to roll this year forward,
settle it among the others

then scramble back down
to see what comes next.

Like many people who grow up to be writers, **Deborah Rasmussen** began at an early age. She remembers showing poems to her second-grade teacher, relishing Mrs. Shepherd's enthusiastic encouragement. Deborah published her first poem at age 11 in a small-town weekly newspaper.

In later school years, Deborah savored the camaraderie of fellow students who loved to write. She continued to write poems, but also began to try out different forms of writing, including short stories and non-fiction. During her career as a registered nurse, Deborah published articles in nursing and other medically oriented literature. When she became a parent, she enjoyed exploring children's literature so much that she wrote and published stories of her own. Her work has appeared in various publications including *Highlights for Children, Cricket,* and *Chicken Soup for the Kid's Soul* (Health Communications, Inc., 1998).

Poetry had slipped into the background until Deborah retired from nursing in 2012 and moved with her husband from Jacksonville, Florida, to Duluth, Minnesota. She had hoped to write a middle grade novel in retirement but instead, through her introduction to the local writing community—and somewhat to her surprise—she rediscovered poetry. Since then, Deborah's poems have appeared in *The Talking Stick, The Thunderbird Review, Barstow & Grand, Rattle Poets Respond®* and on the Lake Superior Writers website among other publications.

The beauty of northern Minnesota and the company of fellow writers in Duluth provide rich inspiration for poems as memories comingle with the joys and challenges of the present. Deborah remains grateful to the teacher who, so long ago, always encouraged her to write.

www.ingramcontent.com/pod-product-compliance
Lightning Source LLC
Chambersburg PA
CBHW022104080426

42734CB00009B/1482